National Curriculum
Key Stage 1 Age 6–7

Practice Papers

Key Stage 1 National Tests

ENGLISH: WRITING

How the Key Stage 1 National Tests will affect your child

- All pupils in Year 2 (age 6–7) will take National Tests and Tasks in English and Mathematics. These important tests and tasks are held between January and June each year and are designed to be an objective assessment of the work your child will have done during Key Stage 1 of the National Curriculum.

- Pupils will also have their school work assessed by their teachers. These teacher assessments will be set alongside your child's results in the National Tests to give a clear picture of his/her overall achievement.

- In July, the results of your child's tests and tasks, together with the teacher assessments, will be reported to you.

How this book will help your child

- This book offers plenty of practice in the type of question your child will face in the Key Stage 1 National Test for English: Writing.

- The answers and a mark scheme have been provided to allow you to check how your child has done.

- Advice is given on how to improve your child's answers and avoid common mistakes.

- A unique Marking grid allows you to record your child's results and estimate the level of the National Curriculum at which he/she is working.

Contents

What you need to know about the National Tests 4
Preparing and practising for the English Tests 6
The Writing Tasks and Tests: A Parent's Overview 8

The Writing Task
A Parent's Guide 9
Planning Sheet: Letter of thanks 12
Planning Sheet: Recipe 13
Extra Practice 14
The Writing Task 16

The Spelling Test
A Parent's Guide 19
The Spelling Test: Part 1 20
The Spelling Test: Part 2 22

The Handwriting Task
A Parent's Guide 24
Handwriting Task 24

Assessing the overall Writing level 25
Performance criteria for assessing Levels 1–3 26
Annotated examples of children's writing: Fiction 28
Annotated examples of children's writing: Non-fiction 35

Detachable section
Contents 1
Story: The Breakfast Pops with Extra Pop! 2
Recipe: Sausage Boats 4
Spelling Test: At the Park 5

What you need to know about the National Tests

What is the purpose of National Tests?

The tests taken by pupils in Year 2 have several functions:

- they provide the government with a snapshot picture of attainment throughout the country, enabling it to make judgements about whether standards are improving nationally;
- they give information to OFSTED about schools' achievements, so that they can judge which schools are improving and which are deemed to be failing their pupils;
- they give you information about what your child has learned and about his/her progress compared to national standards;
- although the results are not used by teachers to determine which class your child will move up into, they do provide the next teacher with an idea of your child's overall attainment.

How do the tests work?

Between January and June of Year 2, your child will be given tasks and tests on the core subjects of English and Mathematics. Progress in Science is based on children's performance throughout Key Stage 1 according to teacher assessment. The tests are carried out under the supervision of teachers in school and are marked by a teacher, too. The results are then brought together for comparison by external moderators and marks are translated into "levels". The level that each mark corresponds to is decided according to results gained in pre-tests and the tests themselves – it varies slightly from year to year.

Once the school has the final collated results of the children's tasks and tests, the results are reported to parents by the end of July. You will also receive the results of classroom assessments made by the teachers based on the work your child has done during the school year. In addition, you will be given a summary of the overall results for the other children in the school and for children nationally. This will tell you how well your child is doing compared with other children of the same age. The school's report will explain what the results show about your child's progress and his/her strengths, particular achievements and targets for development. It will also tell you how to follow up the results with teachers and explain why the task and test results may differ from their assessments.

What do the tests assess?

The tests are designed to assess your child's knowledge, skills and understanding in the context of the programme of study set out in the National Curriculum. This can be found on the National Curriculum website, www.nc.uk.net. The programme of study is divided into three sections, called Attainment Targets (ATs). The first, En1 – Speaking and Listening, is assessed only by the teacher in the classroom, not in written tests. The other two ATs are:

- En2 – Reading;
- En3 – Writing.

The National Curriculum for English defines the level descriptions for each of the three targets, and the test papers have questions covering En2 and En3. Spelling is tested through the child's independent writing and through a Spelling Test. Handwriting is assessed through the Writing Task, or through the child copying out some independent writing in his/her very best handwriting, for the teacher to assess.

What are the levels and what do they mean?

There is a set of benchmark standards that measure a child's progress through the first three Key Stages of the National Curriculum. Attainment is measured in steps, called "levels", from 1 to 7. The National Curriculum document sets out the knowledge, skills and understanding that pupils should demonstrate at each level. The government target is for pupils to achieve Level 2 at the end of Key Stage 1, Level 4 at the end of Key Stage 2 and Level 5 or 6 at the end of Key Stage 3. The chart below shows these government targets.

How your child should progress

There are different Key Stage 1 National Tasks and Tests for different attainment levels. This is to ensure that pupils can undertake a task or test where they can show positive achievement and that they are not too discouraged by trying to answer questions that are too easy or too difficult.

How does this book help my child?

This book gives your child practice in answering the type of question that he/she will take in the actual tests. By practising questions in this way, your child will feel under less pressure and be more relaxed. Being relaxed helps pupils to perform at their best in tests, so we have targeted the questions at Levels 2–3, allowing your child to become familiar with most of the types of question that are asked in the tests. We have also included some guidance on how to assess Gifted and Talented children. This assesses those children who are secure in Level 3 and are working closely towards Level 4. Do not worry if your child cannot achieve this level, as if he/she can reach Level 3, then this is already above the majority of children of his/her age.

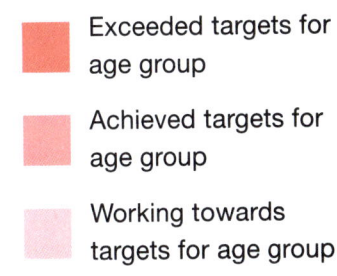
Exceeded targets for age group

Achieved targets for age group

Working towards targets for age group

How your child should progress

Preparing and practising for the English Tests

The questions in this book test the same things as the actual test papers; the Key Stage 1 curriculum for English: Writing.

What are the key features of this book?

This book contains all you need to prepare your child for the tests:

- Questions – writing and handwriting tasks and a Spelling Test.
- Answers – showing the kinds of responses that will gain credit in the tests and how the levels are assessed.
- Guidance for parents – tips and suggestions to help your child improve his/her performance.
- Level charts – what the assessments mean in terms of National Curriculum levels.

How should I use this book?

Allow your child as much time as he/she requires for all the tasks and tests (this is what will happen in school). The tasks and tests should be carried out somewhere your child feels comfortable and he/she should only do one test at a time.

Details of how to approach each test are given at the beginning of each section.

After your child has completed the test, use the assessment guide at the end of each section to assess your child's level. For the Spelling Tests, work out the total marks gained for each question and add them up to arrive at the total mark for each test. You can then use the charts in the marking sections to determine the level of your child's performance in the tests.

What does the level mean?

The tasks and tests in this book give a guide as to the level that your child is likely to achieve in the actual tests. We hope that, through practice, these tests will give your child the confidence to achieve his/her best.

So that you can compare your child's achievement with national standards, the chart opposite shows the percentage of pupils awarded each level in a typical year.

How do I help my child prepare to take the actual tests?

As the tests approach, make sure that your child is as relaxed and confident as possible; remind him/her of the need to concentrate, but also give encouragement to make the tests as enjoyable as possible. Remember, at this age most children won't be aware that they are taking formal tests.

Look out for signs of anxiety in your child. Although many children are perfectly at ease with tests, some do get nervous beforehand. Reassure your child that, though important, the tests and tasks are not the only means by which pupils are assessed.

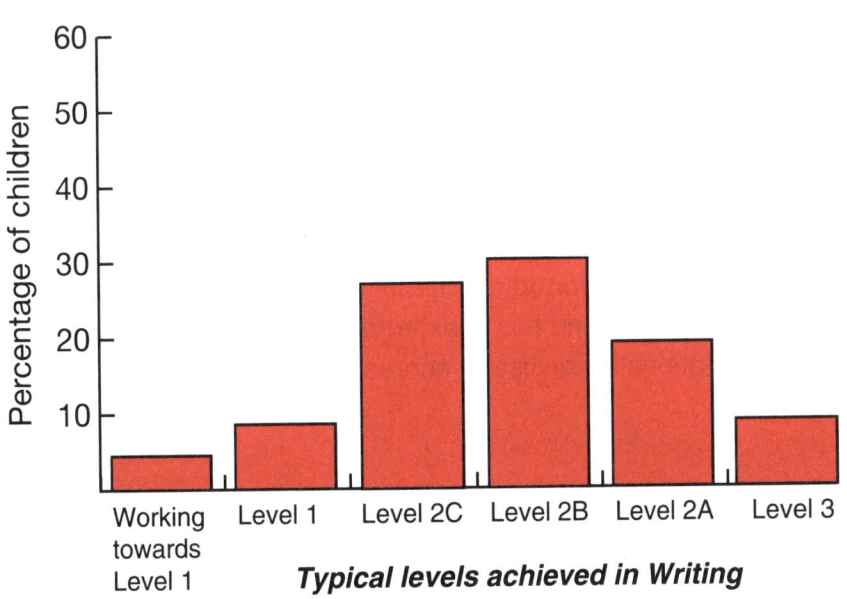

Typical levels achieved in Writing

The Writing Tasks and Tests
Levels 1–3

A PARENT'S OVERVIEW

The tasks and tests are designed to assess your child's attainment in the three areas of En3 – Writing at Key Stage 1, these being:

- writing
- spelling
- handwriting.

Below you will find an explanation of what the assessment of each of these areas involves.

Writing

Children of all abilities will be asked to complete two independent pieces of writing. Criteria and examples of other children's writing are provided to help you assess your child's level. The writing may take a variety of forms, but will include one piece of fiction and one piece of non-fiction.

Spelling

Your child's spelling will be assessed in two ways:

1. from his or her independent writing;
2. from a Spelling Test.

Criteria are provided for you to assess the level of your child's spelling in his or her independent writing in the Performance Criteria For Assessing Levels 1–3 on pages 26 and 27. The Spelling Test is marked as either right or wrong and a level awarded.

Handwriting

Your child may be asked to copy several sentences from his or her own writing, which may be extracted from the Writing Task. Criteria and examples of other children's handwriting are provided to help you assess your child's level.

Assessment

These three areas of En3 – Writing are not assessed separately, but together, when all three tests have been completed. However, a separate spelling level from the Spelling Test is reported to parents as additional information. Marking is carried out by the teacher and this is externally moderated by an assessment officer to ensure nationally consistent scores.

The Writing Task

A PARENT'S GUIDE

The Writing Task is carried out by all children in the final year of Key Stage 1. It is designed to assess how well your child can convey meaning and how accurately he or she can use some of the conventions of writing, such as spelling, punctuation and handwriting.

The Writing Task is divided into two sections:

1 fiction
2 non-fiction.

Fiction

In your child's class, the teacher will decide which approach to writing will best suit the children taking the test, allowing them to demonstrate their highest attainment. The style of writing required of the children will come under one of the headings below.

A personal account This would be inspired by something that took place in a book that your child has read together with you or the teacher. For example: the day I went to the hospital or my trip to the beach.

Informative writing This would be a database entry. For example: facts about sea creatures; an information text about America.

Instructions This would be an explanation of how to do or make something. For example: how to make a 'worm and cheese sandwich'.

Extending and adapting ideas or language patterns This would be i) a further episode in a given story or ii) using the same characters from a story, but in a different setting, or iii) using a repeated phrase.

Letter writing This would be a letter to characters in a story or perhaps a letter to the author or publisher.

Personal responses/review This would be a comment on a book. For example, a short book review.

Expressing opinions This would be giving personal viewpoints. For example, writing about whether traditional or modern houses are best.

Your child's teacher will choose carefully a book to read to the children. She will choose it according to the focus she would like the writing to take. The children will then be expected to write a piece based on the text.

WHAT TO DO

In this instance, a text is provided for you to read to your child, the writing focus of which will be letter writing.

Reading and responding to the text

Use scissors to cut out the story *The Breakfast Pops with Extra Pop!* on pages 2 and 3 of the detachable section of this book.

- Read the story to your child, discuss it and ask the following questions. (Your child can read the story if he or she wants.)

    1. What happened to the Breakfast Pops on the day when the machinery that made them went wrong?
    2. What happened to the people who ate them that day?
    3. How did some people stop themselves from floating up into the sky?
    4. What was wrong with the cakes the children baked in school that day?
    5. How did the man trapped on the school roof finally get down?
    6. How do you think this man felt when his feet touched the ground again?

Explaining the task

- Tell your child to pretend that he/she is the man who was helped down from the school roof by eating the rock cakes. He/she is to write a letter of thanks to the child who threw him the rock cakes.

Planning the writing

- Ask your child to think about his/her writing and what he/she is going to include. Ask him/her to fill out the planning sheet on page 12 as a means of structuring his/her writing.

Using the Planning Sheet

- How will you start your letter?
- How will you thank the child for getting you down to safety?
- How did you feel as you clung on to the school roof?
- What could you see from up there?
- How did the cake taste?
- How will you end the letter?

Writing the letter

Once your child has completed his/her planning, he/she should begin writing the letter, either on the Writing Task pages 16–18 or on a separate piece of paper. Your child should write independently, making his/her best guess at spellings he/she does not know. Remind your child before he/she begins about the importance of using punctuation to make the meaning clear.

Non-fiction

As with the fiction writing, in your child's class the teacher will decide which approach to writing will best suit the child taking the test, allowing him/her to demonstrate his/her best work.

Typical styles of writing are as follows:

- Writing instructions. For example, getting to school, playing a game or writing recipes.
- Note-taking. For example, making simple notes from non-fiction texts, using headings, sub-headings and captions.
- Report writing. For example, writing a report about something they have read, using appropriate language to present, sequence and categorise ideas.

What to do

In this instance, a text is provided for you to read to your child. The focus will be writing instructions. Cut out the recipe from the detachable section of this book (page 4).

- Read the recipe for Sausage Boats with your child. Pay particular attention to the sections into which the recipe is separated.
- Ask your child to write a recipe for a favourite sandwich, following the same format as for the Sausage Boats.

Planning the writing

- Ask your child to use the planning sheet on page 13 to organise his/her writing.

Writing the recipe

- Once your child has completed the planning sheet, he/she should begin writing the recipe, either on the Writing task pages 16–18 or on a separate piece of paper. Your child should write independently, making his/her best guess at spellings he/she does not know. Remind your child before he/she begins about the importance of using punctuation to make the meaning clear.

What writing aids may my child use?

Your child should be allowed to use a variety of aids, provided this is done independently. You should, in fact, provide no direct help once he or she has begun. Aids may include: a word book, a dictionary, a children's thesaurus or any words displayed around the room. However, if your child uses such an aid, you must mark the word for which help was needed with the letter 'H'. (This is to ensure that you do not take these words into account when assessing your child's spelling.)

Do not encourage your child to look up every word he or she is unable to spell. Otherwise, your child will lose the flow of what he/she is writing and become bored. It is far better, and more informative, if children 'have a go' at a spelling by using strategies they have been taught – for example, by saying the word slowly to themselves and sounding it out phonetically.

PLANNING SHEET
Letter of thanks

Think about:
- how to start your letter
- how to end your letter

Write down what you are thanking the child for.

Write down how you felt being stuck on the roof.

Write down 3 things you could see from the school roof.

How did the cake taste?

PLANNING SHEET
Recipe

Preparation time

Cooking time

Number of people it will serve

Ingredients

Method

EXTRA PRACTICE

In addition to these writing tasks, you may encourage your child to write in other styles. Look back to page 9 to see a list of styles your child may choose.

Further tips to improve your child's writing are as follows.

1. **The right style** Help your child to understand how to choose an appropriate style of writing. This depends partly on whom the writing is intended for. A letter to a friend can be chatty and informal, while a letter to a children's newspaper or magazine is likely to be more formal. It also depends on purpose. For example, depending on the subject, a story may set out to stir the reader's imagination, or it may be intended to present a realistic account of certain events.

2. **Planning what to say** Before your child begins to write, make sure that he/she has carefully planned what to say in advance.

3. **Punctuation** Make sure that your child understands the importance of punctuation in helping the reader to make sense of a passage of writing. Sentences need to begin with a capital letter and end with a full stop, or a question mark when appropriate. Some children may be ready to use speech marks, but this is not a requirement at Key Stage 1. You can check with your child's teacher what the children are expected to be able to do and what is a reasonable expectation for your child.

4. **Handwriting** Handwriting should be neat and tidy, and letters of a uniform size. Your child should be able to form all letters correctly, and write them in the correct place on the line. Depending on school policy, your child may be learning joined-up writing. Check with the teacher to find out what the school policy is, in order to ensure that what you tell your child backs up what he or she is learning at school. School policies are not all the same!

5. **Writing Stories** A handy way of helping your child to prepare to do this is to get him or her to plan under three separate headings: plot, characters and setting. Then advise your child about the three basic elements:

    a **Plot**
    Decide what is going to happen. Ensure that the story has a clearly defined beginning, middle and end by working out how the problem or event starts, what situation the characters find themselves in and how it is all resolved.

    b **Characters**
    Decide what characters you are going to have in your story and what sort of people they are. What will they be called? What kind of people will they be? (Here you could add the advice of the children's writer Roald Dahl, 'Make your characters extraordinary'.)

    c **Setting**
    Ask yourself where your story is going to take place.

Next, point out that opening sentences are crucial, and that if a writer does not catch the reader's attention at the beginning, it may be lost for good.

Mention also that a writer should include detail in a piece of writing, as it helps the reader to picture the scene clearly and understand what is happening.

Discuss with your child the need to make sure that what happens in his or her writing is in a logical order.

Ask your child to try to think of sentences that will be interesting for the reader, for example by avoiding repetition. Sentences that continually begin 'And then...', soon become boring to read. Also, you could suggest examples of interesting ways of joining short sentences, such as: '... when all of a sudden...'; or '... and the next thing he knew...'.

Your child should try and use a selection of interesting vocabulary when writing. A good idea is that your child should keep a little notebook of new words encountered in his or her own reading for future use when writing.

If your child chooses to write a story, explain to him or her the importance of keeping to the same narrative form all the way through. If the story begins in the third person ('He' or 'She'), then it must not suddenly change to the first person ('I'). This is quite a common mistake among children of this age.

Similarly, your child must take care to keep his or her story in the same tense. If the story begins in the past tense, then it must continue in this way.

6 **Checking** Always encourage your child to read through what he or she has written very carefully before finishing in order to correct any mistakes, or to refine the style. You may like to suggest that your child looks for repeated words and thinks of appropriate alternatives.

The Writing Task

The Writing Task

The Writing Task

The Spelling Test

A PARENT'S GUIDE

This Spelling Test is designed to be carried out by all children working within Levels 2 and 3. Its purpose is to provide a spelling level as well as additional information concerning your child's spelling, which will contribute to his/her final writing level.

The advantage of the Spelling Test is that it provides a sample of your child's spelling that concentrates specifically on that, as opposed to any other aspect of writing. There are two parts to the Spelling Test:

1 **a picture:** your child has to spell correctly the words for some of the items in that picture

2 **a passage:** your child has to fill in the missing words as you read the passage slowly to him/her.

Each target word is allowed 2 marks: one is awarded for writing the initial letter(s) correctly and the other for spelling the whole word correctly. Sometimes a blend of *two* initial letters is required to achieve the mark for the initial letter.

What to do

There is no time limit for this test.

Your child should not receive any help with any spellings.

SPELLING TEST: PART 1

Look at the picture on pages 20–21 together with your child and make sure that he or she knows what all the pictures represent.

Ask your child to attempt the practice question. Then check the answer together and make sure he/she has spelt it correctly. The target word is 'pens'.

Now ask your child to fill in the correct words in the boxes by the pictures.
The target words are:

> **children   door   blind   clock   toilet   books   poster   carpet   shelf   sink**

You may remind your child what each picture is, if necessary.

When your child has completed part 1 of the Spelling Test, add up his or her score by using the key below, and fill in the number of marks awarded in the box on page 21, excluding the practice question.

The School: Part 1 Question	Answer	Mark (initial letter[s])	Mark (whole word)	Total marks	Question	Answer	Mark (initial letter[s])	Mark (whole word)	Total marks
practice	pens	practice	practice						
1	children	1 (*ch*)	1	(2 marks)	6	books	1 (*b*)	1	(2 marks)
2	door	1 (*d*)	1	(2 marks)	7	poster	1 (*p*)	1	(2 marks)
3	blind	1 (*bl*)	1	(2 marks)	8	carpet	1 (*c*)	1	(2 marks)
4	clock	1 (*cl*)	1	(2 marks)	9	shelf	1 (*sh*)	1	(2 marks)
5	toilet	1 (*t*)	1	(2 marks)	10	sink	1 (*s*)	1	(2 marks)

The Spelling Test

Part 1

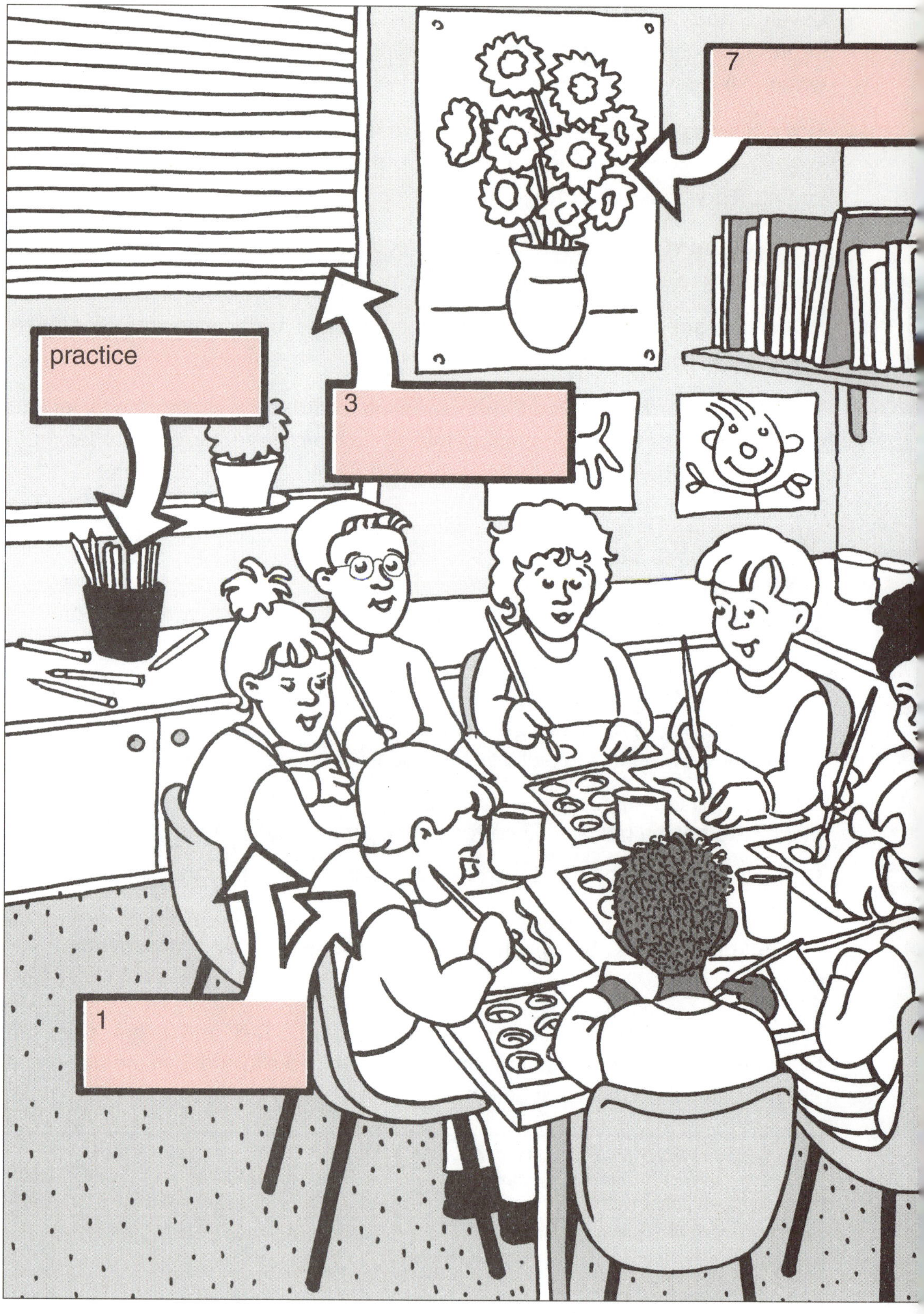

practice

7

3

1

The Spelling Test

The Spelling Test

SPELLING TEST: PART 2

Turn to page 5 of the detachable section of this book, where you will find a passage from a story entitled *At the Park*. Use scissors to cut along the guideline. This is for your child to complete.

Ask your child to follow the passage on the sheet, while you read the complete passage on page 23. Read the passage through at a speed that will allow your child to follow.

Ask your child to notice that some of the words are missing on his or her sheet. Explain that you will read the passage again, more slowly this time, pausing at the gaps to allow your child to fill in the missing words. The first word is for practice. You may wish to get your child to use a pencil so that he or she can try again at a later stage.

The words in bold type are the target words.

Begin the test. You may repeat the target words once.

When your child has completed part 2 of the Spelling Test, add up the total score (excluding the practice question) and write this in the box on page 6 of the detachable section.

SPELLING TEST SCORE

Add together the scores for parts 1 and 2 of the Spelling Test and fill in the score in the box below.

Take this score into account when assessing your child's overall level for Writing.

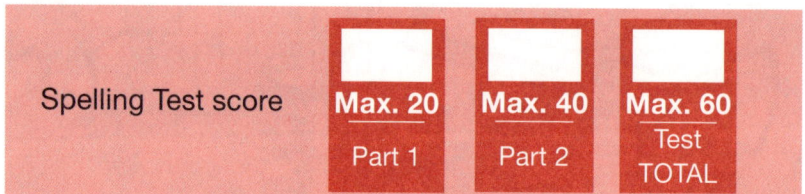

What to do with this score

Number of marks	0–16	17–30	31–48	49–60
Level	Level 1 not achieved	Level 1 achieved	Level 2 achieved	Level 3 achieved

To work out your child's overall level for spelling, refer to the chart below.

The Spelling Test

Part 2

AT THE PARK

It was a sunny day and the **park** was crowded. Children were running **around** and playing.

A **group** of women were sitting on the grass near the park bench, chatting; two dogs were **leaping** around chasing sticks; a group of boys were playing **tennis**; a crowd of children were playing **football** with their **parents** – a perfect **sight** on a sunny summer's day. All of a sudden, a scream arose from the area where the slide was situated. A **little** girl, whose name was Ilona, had fallen from the bottom of the slide and had broken her arm. Immediately, one of the women by the bench took her **mobile** telephone from her handbag, and rang 999. The girl's **friends** ran to be with their parents, **while** Ilona was comforted by her **father**.

Within a few **minutes**, an **ambulance** arrived on the scene, and Ilona was bundled in and taken straight to the hospital.

It was sunny **again** the next day and the park was **once** more full of children. **People** were talking about the events of the day before, when suddenly, the park gate swung open, and Ilona appeared, **sporting** an arm in plaster. All of her friends ran towards her, wanting to know what had happened. Before Ilona had a chance to speak, her plaster was covered in an array of kind messages from her friends. Ilona was so pleased with her plaster!

Perhaps it hadn't been so bad **breaking** her arm, after all!

Question	Answer	Mark (initial letter[s])	Mark (whole word)	Total marks	Question	Answer	Mark (initial letter[s])	Mark (whole word)	Total marks
practice	park	practice	practice						
1	around	1 (*a*)	1	(2 marks)	11	while	1 (*wh*)	1	(2 marks)
2	group	1 (*gr*)	1	(2 marks)	12	father	1 (*f*)	1	(2 marks)
3	leaping	1 (*l*)	1	(2 marks)	13	minutes	1 (*m*)	1	(2 marks)
4	tennis	1 (*t*)	1	(2 marks)	14	ambulance	1 (*a*)	1	(2 marks)
5	football	1 (*f*)	1	(2 marks)	15	again	1 (*a*)	1	(2 marks)
6	parents	1 (*p*)	1	(2 marks)	16	once	1 (*o*)	1	(2 marks)
7	sight	1 (*s*)	1	(2 marks)	17	people	1 (*p*)	1	(2 marks)
8	little	1 (*l*)	1	(2 marks)	18	sporting	1 (*sp*)	1	(2 marks)
9	mobile	1 (*m*)	1	(2 marks)	19	perhaps	1 (*p*)	1	(2 marks)
10	friends	1 (*fr*)	1	(2 marks)	20	breaking	1 (*br*)	1	(2 marks)

The Handwriting Task

A PARENT'S GUIDE

The Handwriting Task can take a variety of forms. At school, the teacher may assess your child's handwriting by carefully examining it in the Writing Task, or may ask your child to copy something out in his/her best handwriting. However it is assessed, it ultimately forms part of the overall assessment for Writing.

In this book, we suggest that you take a few sentences from the Writing Task, and ask your child to copy them out in his/her best handwriting.

What to do

- Together with your child, choose approximately three sentences from his or her writing.
- Ask your child to copy them on to the lines underneath in his or her very best handwriting.
- Take this example of your child's handwriting into account when assessing your child's overall writing level, by using the criteria provided on pages 26–27.

My best handwriting

Assessing the overall Writing level

To assess your child's overall level, you need to take into account your child's Writing Task (in itself displaying techniques of spelling and handwriting), and also the specific Spelling Test and Handwriting Task.

To do this, you will need to refer very closely to the performance criteria described on pages 26–27 for each level, which are directly related to the National Curriculum Orders for English.

You will notice that Level 2 is banded into three groups: 2A, 2B and 2C – 2A being the highest and 2C the lowest. This is because Level 2 is the level attained by the majority of children and yet within this level quite a range of achievement is possible.

Owing to the nature of written language, it is not possible simply to fill in tick lists as an effective form of assessment. Therefore, you will need to read carefully the specific criteria for each level and decide which performance description fits your child best. This is known as a 'best fit' judgement. To ensure that you are picking the 'best fit', always make sure you read the criteria for the levels directly above and below as a comparison. Look at the criteria in a balanced way; do not cloud your judgement by regarding one criterion as more important or weighty than another. It is not necessary to meet all the criteria to attain a level and some aspects of your child's writing may reflect the level above or below the one which you judge to be the best fit. This is common and should not be regarded as a problem.

To help you make your assessments, you will find examples of children's writing on pages 28–40, with notes as to why a particular level was attributed.

Assessing the overall Writing level

PERFORMANCE CRITERIA FOR ASSESSING LEVELS 1–3

Level 1

- Simple words and phrases are used.
- The writing has some appropriate use of capital letters and full stops.
- Letters are usually clearly shaped and usually start and finish in the correct place.

Level 2C

- The writing includes more than a simple statement.
- The overall feel of the writing is of spoken rather than written language.
- Individual ideas are developed in short sections.
- The writing shows some characteristics of the chosen form.
- There is some evidence of full stops and capital letters being used to mark individual sentences or clauses.
- Some common words are spelt correctly; otherwise the child has generally tried to 'sound out' the word or re-create the 'shape' of it (e.g. 'breakfst') .
- The handwriting is legible, although letters may not always be formed correctly. Capitals and small letters may be mixed up and letters may not be of the same size.

Level 2B

- There is some attempt to vary sentence structure and/or word choices.
- Some sentences are linked or extended through the use of words other than 'and'.
- Some elaboration is used to interest the reader.
- Some sentences are punctuated with capital letters and full stops.
- The organisation of the writing reflects the purpose.
- Appropriate writing form is used with some consistency.
- The child draws on a range of strategies to work out the spelling of unfamiliar words: this may include using common patterns (-tion, -opped); 'sounding out' and recreating the 'shape' of a word.
- Handwriting is clear. Letters such as h, t, g and p extend appropriately above or below the line. Capitals and small letters are rarely mixed within a word.

Level 2A

- Descriptive phrases are used to add detail and emphasis.
- Ideas are linked together in clear ways, using a variety of linking words such as 'because' and 'which'.

Assessing the overall Writing level

- Full stops and capital letters are clearly used to mark sentences that are generally correctly structured.
- The writing communicates meaning in a lively way, generally holding the reader's interest.
- Events and comments are clearly linked.
- The chosen form is used appropriately, with awareness of its target audience.
- Spelling of simple (one-syllable) words is accurate. Longer words are plausibly attempted (i.e. the sounds make sense).
- Handwriting is clear, with letters consistently and accurately formed.

Level 3

- Sentences are varied in length and structure, and they are usually grammatically correct.
- Most sentences are correctly punctuated, using capital letters and full stops, and question/exclamation marks where necessary.
- Ideas are logically organised and follow on smoothly.
- The writing is clear and displays imagination (e.g. through the inclusion of appropriate but unusual details).
- The writing is lively and holds the reader's interest.
- Spelling is usually accurate, including that of common words of more than one syllable.
- Handwriting is clear and joined.

Gifted and Talented

- Sentences are varied in length and structure to create effects (e.g. contrast, humour, suspense).
- Sentences are grammatically correct and almost always correctly punctuated, with some use of commas if necessary.
- Links and/or distinctions between sections are clear; there may be some use of paragraphs.
- The body of the writing is well constructed.
- The writing is lively and imaginative, engaging and holding the reader's interest throughout.
- The writing is well organised to suit the purpose and audience.
- Spelling is accurate.
- Handwriting is clear, joined and shows the beginnings of a personal style.

Assessing the overall Writing level

ANNOTATED EXAMPLES OF CHILDREN'S WRITING: FICTION

The following five children were all presented with the same task. They were required to listen to the story of *The Breakfast Pops with Extra Pop!* and to use it as a stimulus for letter writing, as explained on page 10.

Level 1

This child's writing communicates meaning through very simple phrases, mostly unpunctuated with capital letters and full stops, although there is some evidence of punctuation. The letters are clearly shaped, although gaps between words are not sufficient, giving the impression of making no sense. However, when the child read the writing out loud, it became clear where each word began and ended.

> Dir Boy and gl
> thak you for brinin no down
> thaeros. sow theay throo
> sum ka b u p tow t ne w the
> ths an d t wo B) pipol wont to
> tost the kar sow to w wr
> livin withe Bos.
> from nat

Overall, the 'best fit' is assessed as Level 1.

Assessing the overall Writing level

Level 2C

This child's writing communicates meaning beyond the simple statement by the use of some added detail, e.g. "rock hard muffin", and personal experience, e.g. "I did not like it up in the air." The basic features of a letter are used, i.e. "dear …" and "from …", and some sentences address the children directly, although the purpose of other statements is unclear. Capital letters and full stops are sometimes used to clarify meaning, even though the use of capital letters is sometimes arbitrary. The spelling of common words is generally accurate and phonetic attempts make sense. The handwriting is legible, despite some inconsistencies of lower and upper case letters.

> Dear children
> Thank you for the Rook hard mufin Lucky That you throw it up I did not like it up in The air. The pop Breakfast must of whent rong. now They no what went rong. I got down by a Ladder.
>
> from
> Barry

Overall, the 'best fit' is assessed as Level 2C.

Assessing the overall Writing level

Level 2B

This child's writing is appropriate to the letter writing style. She employs a varied vocabulary and sentence structure to engage the reader's attention, drawing on the use of the interactive questioning technique. The content follows a logical progression. Sentences are mostly punctuated correctly. Spelling is almost entirely accurate and the handwriting displays a controlled cursive technique.

> Dear Children
> this morning after eating my Breakfast, do you no what? My Breakfast pops made me flot up up up. Past a Shop. And then a girl came out of your School and threw up some (c) rock hard cakes because she felt sorry for me. But the rock hard cakes made me hevair. (oh) then I said Thank you Thank you. You saved my life. Thank you
> P.S. (ples) (ples) please make me some more.
>
> from m.rs. Jessie.

Overall, the 'best fit' is assessed as Level 2B.

Assessing the overall Writing level

Level 2A

This child's writing shows imagination, using descriptive detail to engage the reader's attention. Although the grammar and spelling are not entirely accurate, the writing is appropriate for an informal letter, with detail included for interest, e.g. "If you hadn't saved me I would be on the moon by now and it was kind of boring up on that chimney." In addition, full stops and capital letters are clearly used to mark correctly structured sentences and the child's handwriting is beautifully clear, with letters consistently and accurately formed.

> Dear children
> Today when I was eating my brekfast pops I felt like I had blown up a berloon and the air had went back in my mouth. And when you gave me the pies I was really healy and I want to thank you for reskuin me. If you hadent savd me I would be on the moon by now and it was kind of boring up on that chimney. But now cro im on the ground I will make shore my feet is on the flor for ever. from mr. and mrs. Sprout
> PS. I no how father christmas fills. now!

Overall, the 'best fit' is assessed as Level 2A.

Assessing the overall Writing level

Level 3

This child's writing is appropriate to the letter writing style. It begins by setting out its purpose: to thank the students for saving him. This is followed by a personal response: "I am very impressed with you." The child then outlines the purpose of the next part of the letter: "I have to tell you a little story", which announces the retelling of events after having eaten the Breakfast Pops with Extra Pop. The child's writing is controlled and the content illustrates good planning. Vocabulary is chosen for variety and interest, displaying a control of language, e.g. instead of saying "I went up to the sky", he says, "I started to head for the sky." The sentences are almost always punctuated accurately with capital letters, full stops and exclamation marks. Spelling is usually accurate and the handwriting is joined and clear.

> Dear Student's
> Thank you for helping me get down from the sky. I am very impressed with you. I have to tell you a little story. I was eating my beakfast when suddenly I took off. I went out off the (Kit) kitchen door into the living room heading for the fire place, bashed into it, went through it, and went up the chimney. The chimney was very long and at last I came out of the other end of the chimney

Assessing the overall Writing level

and I started to head for the sky. I went higher and higher until BUMP! My head hit the clouds! I fell back down to the ground, then I bounced back up to the sky but I caught the roof of your school. Then you came out of the school and threw the cake up to me. I missed the first time you threw the cake up to me. I missed the second time, but not the third time. I ate about ten cakes util I sank down to the ground. That was pretty fun. The cake tasted like (the time) a bowl full of flour. It also reminded me of the time I picked up a bowl of flour and stuffed it down my throt. That's it for now!

Love the man on the roof xx

Overall, the 'best fit' is assessed as Level 3.

Assessing the overall Writing level

Gifted and Talented

This letter is lively and imaginative, engaging and holding the reader's interest throughout. It achieves this by including descriptive detail about the view the letter-writer had from the top of the school roof and also how he felt about the cakes. Sentences are varied in length and structure to create effects and always gramatically correct and correctly punctuated. The letter is well structured and it is separated thematically into paragraphs. The writer has a sense of audience and the style of the letter suits its purpose. Spelling is accurate and the joined handwriting is beginning to demonstrate a personal style.

> Dear William,
>
> I'm very grateful for what you did yesterday. I could've been up on the roof all my life but your class were there to save me.
>
> When I was up on the roof I felt very worried and sick. I felt sick because I was so dizzy. I felt worried because I thought I wouldn't be able to get down to Earth.
>
> Seeing I was high up on the school roof I could see for miles around. I could see the tree tops with all the branches and leaves on top. There were birds nesting in their nests and in the distance I could see a woman grabbing hold of a church steeple. I think she was up there because she had eaten the pops with extra pop.
>
> Helpfully you came and got me down by those cakes that you made. Your teacher thought it was a stupid idea. I could've died of starvation and thirst until I ate the rock cakes. I must admit they

> tasted horrible and I really thought I couldn't or wouldn't come down to the ground. Those cakes tasted very hard be dry and dry, but that doesn't matter. I'm quite fat now because I ate a lot of cakes, but that doesn't matter because it's not my fault, I had to.
>
> When my wife saw me come down she fainted!! You're the brainy one coming up with such a good idea. I don't know what I'd have done without you. Thank you for saving my life.
>
> Yours sincerely,
>
> Harry.

Overall, the 'best fit' is assessed as Level 3*.

Assessing the overall Writing level

ANNOTATED EXAMPLES OF CHILDREN'S WRITING: NON-FICTION

Level 1

This recipe for Marmite sandwiches is conveyed through the use of simple words and phrases. Phonic attempts are made at spelling and there is some appropriate use of capital letters. Letters are correctly formed, starting and finishing in the correct place.

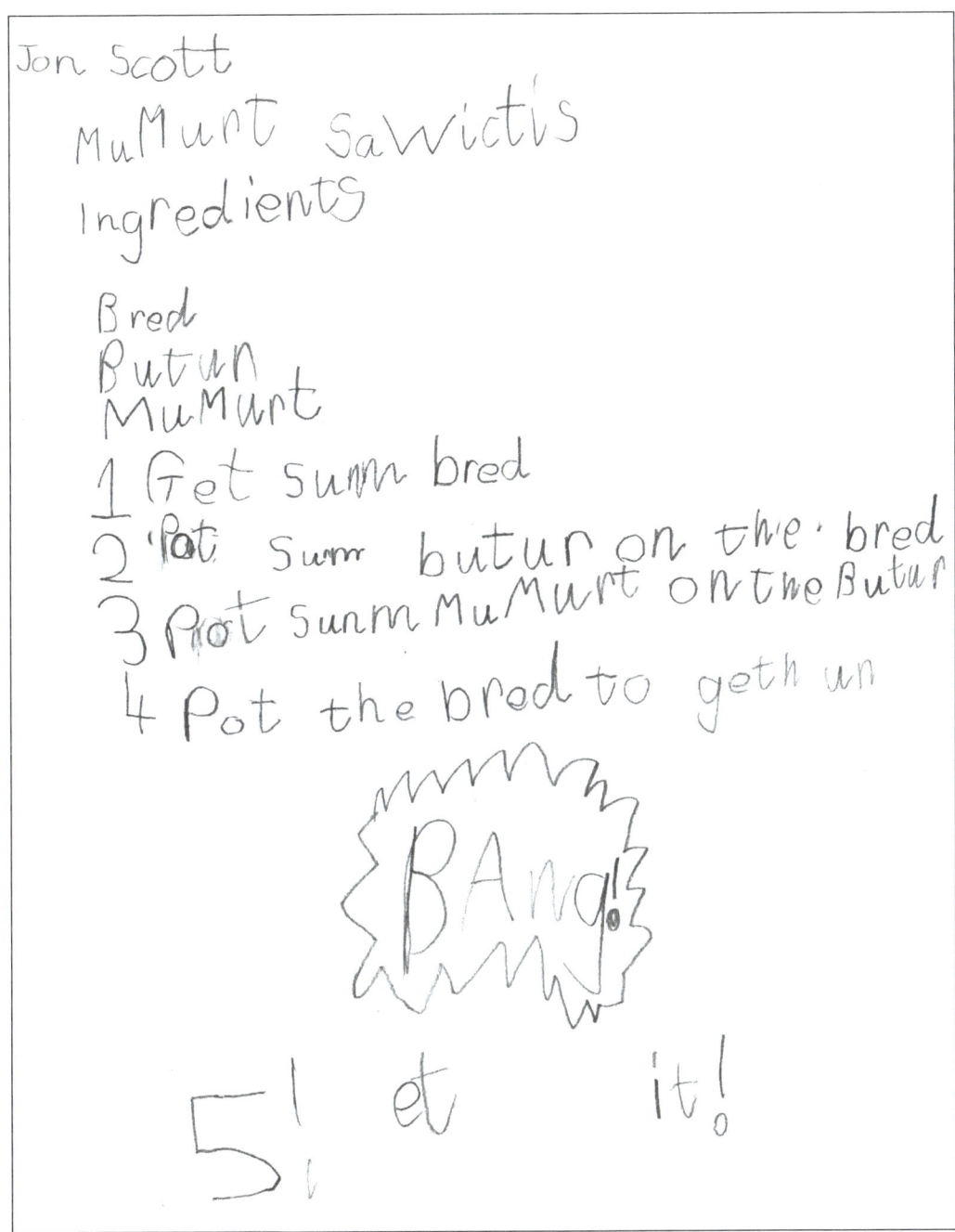

Overall, the 'best fit' is assessed as Level 1.

Assessing the overall Writing level

Level 2C

This recipe is written using more than a simple statement. The ideas are developed chronologically, appropriate to the chosen form. Capital letters and full stops are sometimes used to demarcate sentences. Most common words are spelt correctly; incorrect spellings still display an understanding of spelling patterns, e.g. "peacs" for "pieces". Handwriting is printed and clear, although there is some confusion between upper and lower case letters.

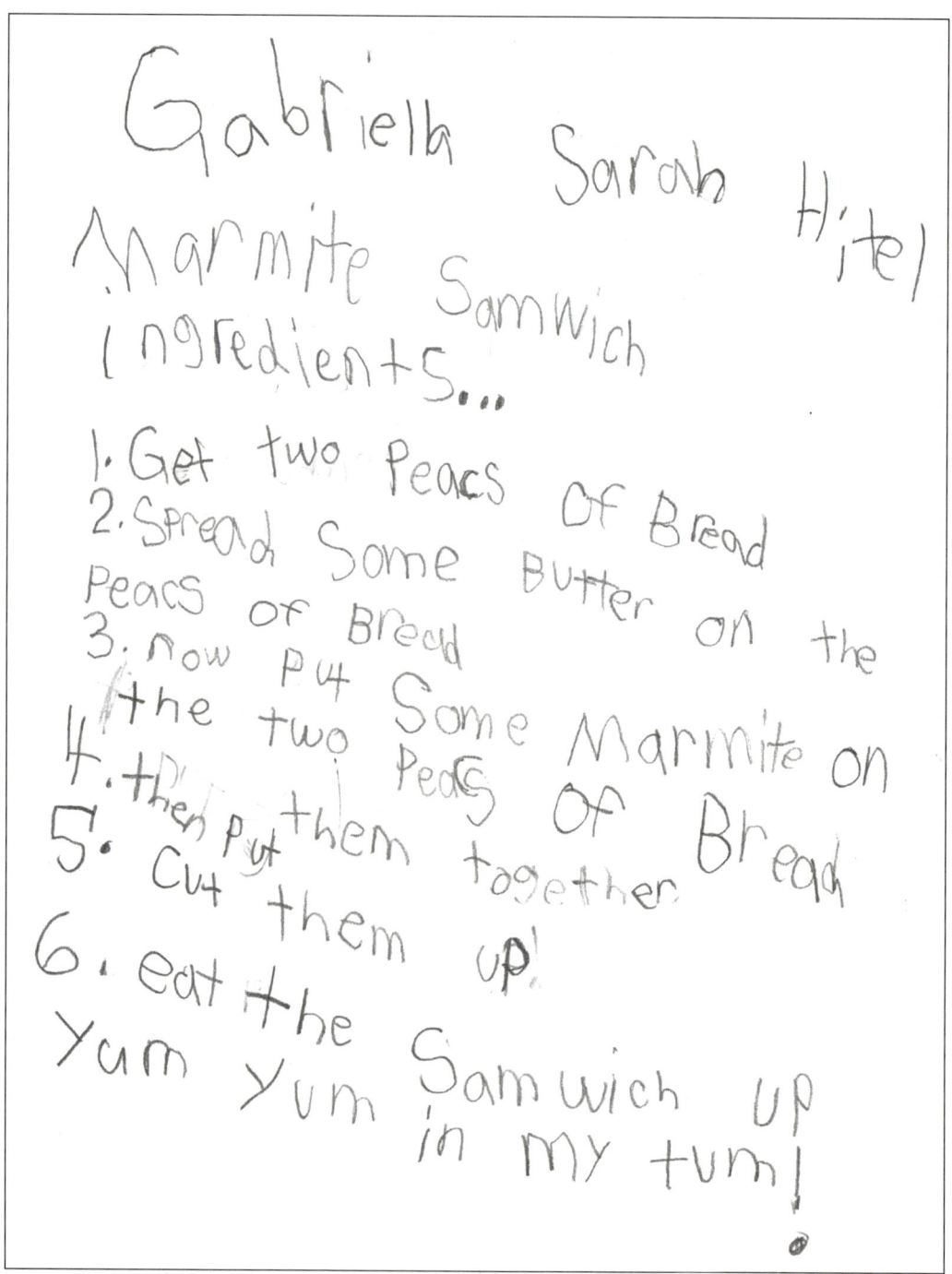

Overall, the 'best fit' is assessed as Level 2C.

Assessing the overall Writing level

Level 2B

This recipe for ham and cheese sandwiches conveys the information clearly and is appropriate to the style of a recipe. Sentences begin with a range of words other than "then", e.g. "First, …" and "Next, …". Sentences always end with full stops and they usually begin with capital letters. Spelling is generally accurate and handwriting is clear. Capitals and small letters are not mixed within a word.

Overall, the 'best fit' is assessed as Level 2B.

Assessing the overall Writing level

Level 2A

The writing in this recipe reflects its purpose. It is well ordered, with descriptive phrases used to add detail and emphasis, e.g. "Pull out three spoonfuls of chocolate." Sentences are consistently well punctuated. Spelling is accurate and handwriting is joined and clear.

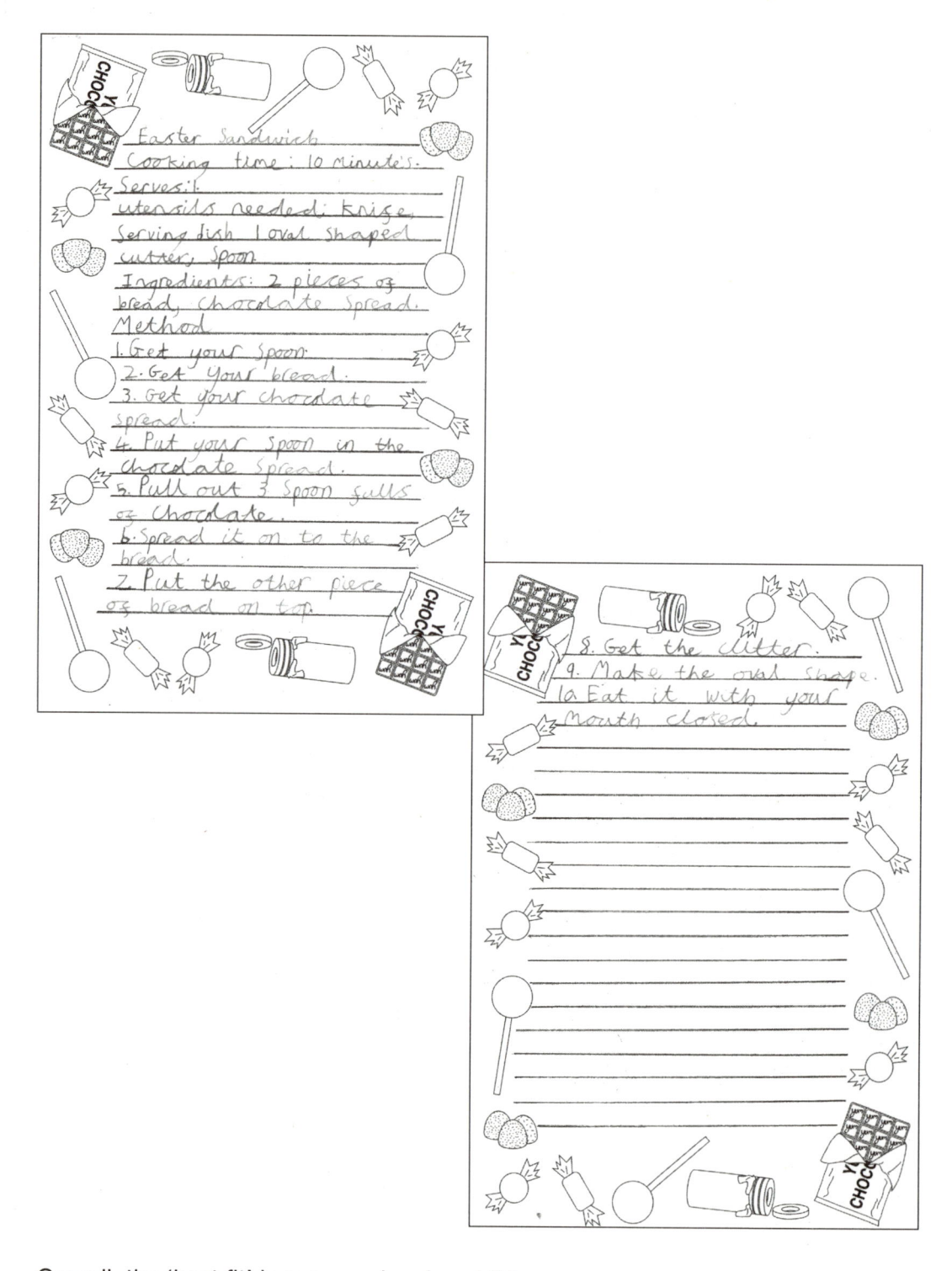

> Easter Sandwich
> Cooking time: 10 minutes.
> Serves: 1
> Utensils needed: knife, serving dish, 1 oval shaped cutter, spoon
> Ingredients: 2 pieces of bread, chocolate spread.
> Method
> 1. Get your spoon.
> 2. Get your bread.
> 3. Get your chocolate spread.
> 4. Put your spoon in the chocolate spread.
> 5. Pull out 3 spoonfulls of chocolate.
> 6. Spread it on to the bread.
> 7. Put the other piece of bread on top.
> 8. Get the cutter.
> 9. Make the oval shape.
> 10. Eat it with your mouth closed.

Overall, the 'best fit' is assessed as Level 2A.

Assessing the overall Writing level

Level 3

This child's writing is logically organised and each stage follows on smoothly from the last. Descriptive detail is used to good effect, e.g. "Lay down the bread on the work surface", and an interesting way of phrasing the sentences engages and holds the reader's interest, e.g. "Stack the squares up into a tower". Sentences are correctly punctuated, using capital letters and full stops. Spelling is accurate and the handwriting is clear and joined.

> Chicken tower sandwich
> Cooking time 10 minutes
> serves 1
> Utensils needed Plate, fork, knife, long cocktail stick.
> Ingredients chicken strips, white bread and mayonnaise.
> Method:
> 1) First lay down the bread on the worksurface and put the chicken strips on the bread and spread the mayonnaise on.
> 2) Next put another piece of bread on top of the first one
> 3) Cut the sandwich into four.
> 4) Stack the squares up into a tower and put the long cocktail stick through.
> 5) It's ready to eat.

Overall, the 'best fit' is assessed as Level 3.

Assessing the overall Writing level

Gifted and Talented

This recipe for toasted cheese sandwiches is well organised and set out according to the conventions of recipe writing. The steps are ordered chronologically, with appropriate attention to detail. Paragraphs are used to good effect, with clear headings. Vocabulary is used precisely to convey information accurately. Sentences are grammatically correct and always correctly punctuated. Spelling is accurate and the cursive handwriting displays a personal style.

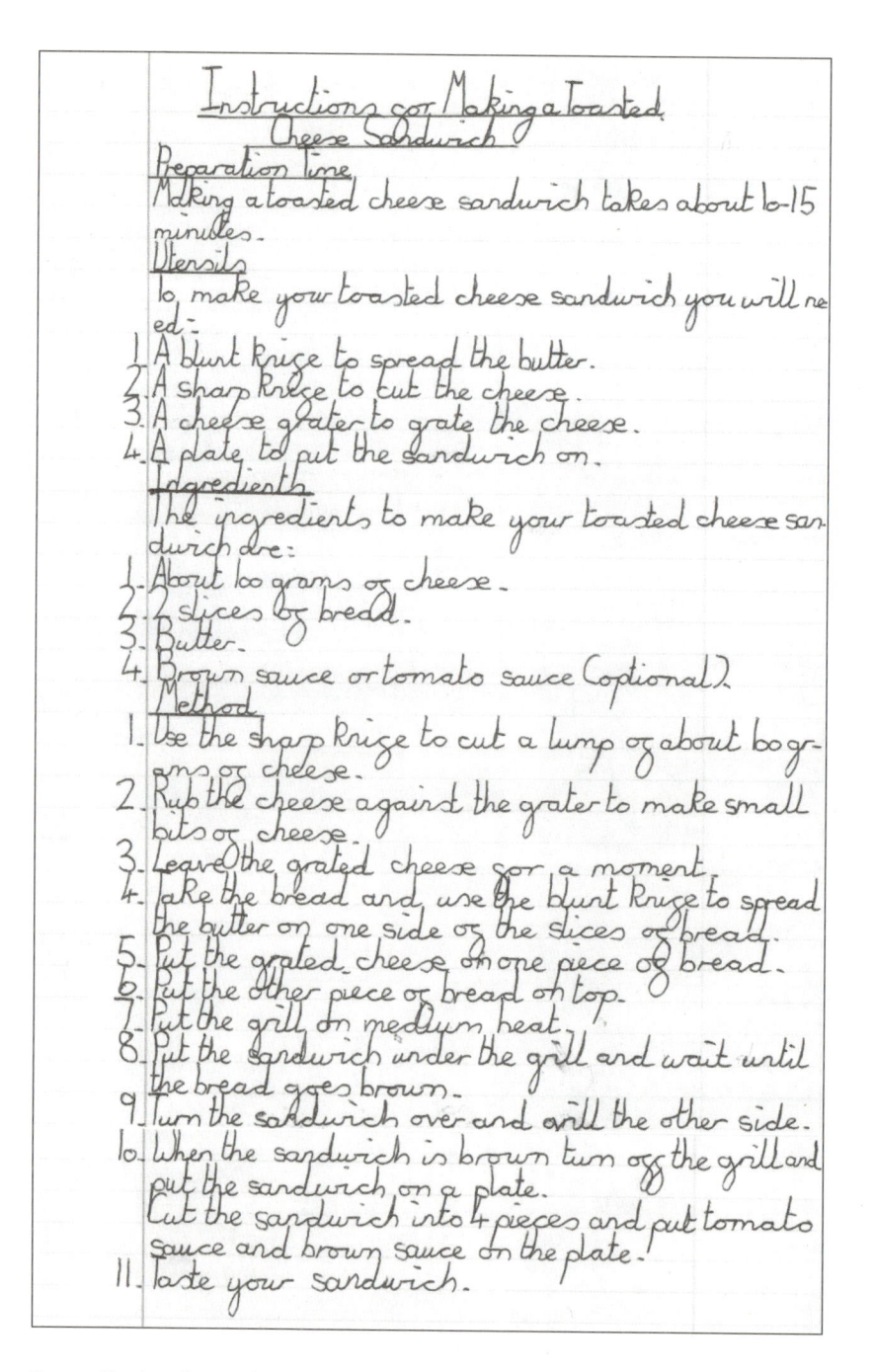

> **Instructions for Making a Toasted Cheese Sandwich**
>
> **Preparation Time**
> Making a toasted cheese sandwich takes about 10-15 minutes.
>
> **Utensils**
> To make your toasted cheese sandwich you will need:
> 1. A blunt knife to spread the butter.
> 2. A sharp knife to cut the cheese.
> 3. A cheese grater to grate the cheese.
> 4. A plate to put the sandwich on.
>
> **Ingredients**
> The ingredients to make your toasted cheese sandwich are:
> 1. About 100 grams of cheese.
> 2. 2 slices of bread.
> 3. Butter.
> 4. Brown sauce or tomato sauce (optional).
>
> **Method**
> 1. Use the sharp knife to cut a lump of about 80 grams of cheese.
> 2. Rub the cheese against the grater to make small bits of cheese.
> 3. Leave the grated cheese for a moment.
> 4. Take the bread and use the blunt knife to spread the butter on one side of the slices of bread.
> 5. Put the grated cheese on one piece of bread.
> 6. Put the other piece of bread on top.
> 7. Put the grill on medium heat.
> 8. Put the sandwich under the grill and wait until the bread goes brown.
> 9. Turn the sandwich over and grill the other side.
> 10. When the sandwich is brown turn off the grill and put the sandwich on a plate. Cut the sandwich into 4 pieces and put tomato sauce and brown sauce on the plate.
> 11. Taste your sandwich.

Overall, the 'best fit' is assessed as Level 3*.

Detachable Section

CONTENTS

Story: The Breakfast Pops with Extra Pop!   2

Recipe: Sausage Boats   4

Spelling Test: At the Park   5

Story

The Breakfast Pops with Extra Pop!

In our town there is a factory where they make Breakfast Pops. TV adverts say it's 'everybody's favourite crunchy cereal', and I'm sure they're right.

Inside the factory there is lots of machinery clinking and clanking, day and night, to make each and every Breakfast Pop round and crunchy and, most importantly, with a proper-sized hole in the middle full of air. This, after all, is the secret of what makes each Breakfast Pop go 'pop!' in your mouth.

We're all very proud of Breakfast Pops in our town and we eat more than most. Well, we did until the awful day when the machines in the factory went wrong. A screw came off a wotsit and fell through a pipe into a thingummyjig, and before anyone could stop it happening, the machines began to put too much air in the holes inside the Breakfast Pops, so they became Breakfast Pops with Extra Pop!

The result was disastrous. Anyone who ate Breakfast Pops with Extra Pop the next morning got a shock. Their stomach filled with air and they began to float upwards like a balloon at a party. Some people grabbed on to trees to stop themselves floating off into the sky. Others missed the trees and floated up helplessly until they bumped into the clouds.

Nobody knew what to do, so the poor breakfast eaters had to stay in the sky for a while. Luckily it wasn't raining but, even so, it wasn't much fun up there. Someone had to find the answer fast, before the whole world saw the story on the TV news and stopped buying Breakfast Pops forever.

We found the answer by accident, and everyone in our school became instant heroes. It was just luck really, because that day we were learning to bake cakes. The teacher said they were

The Breakfast Pops with Extra Pop

supposed to be soft and light. "As fluffy as a pillow," she said. Instead they came out of the oven hard and heavy, more like moon rocks.

"You have all mixed in too much flour!" the teacher complained. "Start again!"

I sighed and looked out of the window, and that's when I saw the man who had eaten Breakfast Pops with Extra Pop. He had grabbed on to the roof of the school as he had floated upwards and now he was hanging on desperately.

"Come down at once!" cried the teacher when she saw him.

"I don't know how to! Any ideas?" the man shouted down.

"Here, have a cake," I cried, and I threw one up to the poor man, because I felt sorry for him.

"Don't eat that! It's rock hard!" the teacher gasped, but he did, and when it got inside his stomach it made him feel heavier.

"This might work!" he cried between mouthfuls, so we threw him another cake, and another, until he was heavy enough to stop floating and sank slowly back down to the ground.

"You saved me!" he cried, and he rushed off to tell everyone what had happened. We set to work baking more cakes. Then we used catapults, tennis racquets and kites to get them to the floating people. One by one they ate enough cakes to sink back down to earth. That's how we saved the honour of our town, our factory and our Breakfast Pops – with no Extra Pop!

Of course, there were one or two fussy eaters, who said they didn't like cake and wouldn't even try a single bite. They're still up there living in the sky with the birds.

I ask you – how fussy can you get?

Recipe

Sausage Boats

Cooking time: 25 minutes

Serves: 4

Utensils needed: fork, knife, grill pan, serving dish

Ingredients: 4 sausages
2 slices of processed cheese
4 cocktail sticks

Method:

1 Turn on the grill to medium heat.

2 Prick the sausages with a fork.

3 Cook the sausages under the grill, turning frequently with a fork, for approximately 20 minutes, or until the sausages are cooked.

4 Cut the slices of processed cheese in 2 diagonally.

5 Attach the cheese to the cocktail sticks as shown in the picture, to form a sail.

6 Push each sail into a sausage.

7 Arrange sausage boats in a serving dish.

8 Eat warm or cold.

Spelling Test

At the Park

It was a sunny day and the .... was crowded. Children were running .... and playing.

A .... of women were sitting on the grass near the park bench, chatting; two dogs were .... around chasing sticks; a group of boys were playing .... ; a crowd of children were playing .... with their .... – a perfect .... on a sunny summer's day. All of a sudden, a scream arose from the area where the slide was situated. A .... girl, whose name was Ilona, had fallen from the bottom of the slide and had broken her arm. Immediately, one of the women by the bench took her .... telephone from her handbag, and rang 999. The girl's .... ran to be with their parents, ... Ilona was comforted by her ....

Within a few .... , an .... arrived

At the Park

on the scene, and Ilona was bundled in and taken straight to the hospital.

It was sunny …………… the next day and the park was …………… more full of children. …………… were talking about the events of the day before, when suddenly, the park gate swung open, and Ilona appeared, …………… an arm in plaster. All of her friends ran towards her, wanting to know what had happened. Before Ilona had a chance to speak, her plaster was covered in an array of kind messages from her friends. Ilona was so pleased with her plaster!

…………… it hadn't been so bad …………… her arm, after all!

Letts

Practice Papers

Key Stage 1 National Tests

ENGLISH: WRITING

The test questions and answers contained in this publication are based upon the official test materials provided to schools, but do not reproduce those tests exactly. The official tests are supported by administrative and other guidance for teachers to use in setting the tests, marking them, and interpreting their results. The results your child achieves in taking the tests in this book may not be the same as what he/she achieves in the official tests.

Every effort has been made to trace copyright holders and to obtain their permission for the use of copyright material. The author and publishers will gladly receive any information enabling them to rectify any error or omission in subsequent editions.

First published 1997
Reprinted 1997, 1999
Revised 1997, 1998, 1999, 2000, 2001, 2002
Reprinted 2002

Text: © Letts Educational Ltd 1999, 2002
Author: Sarah Harris
The publishers are grateful to Sally Manz for authenticating the contents.

Design and illustrations:
© Letts Educational Ltd 2000, 2002

All our Rights Reserved. No part of this publication may be reproduced, stored in a retrieval system or transmitted, in any form or by any means, electronic, mechanical, photocopying, recording or otherwise, without the prior permission of Letts Educational.
British Library Cataloguing in Publication Data
A CIP record for this book is available from the British Library.

ISBN: 1 84315 057 3

Cover design by 2idesign, Cambridge
Cover logo by Starfish Design for Print, London
Project management and typesetting by Cambridge Publishing Management

Printed in Italy.

Acknowledgements
The author and publishers wish to thank the children of Year 2, Waltham Holy Cross Infant School, Waltham Abbey, Essex, for participating in the preparation of this book, and Moira Butterfield for her story, *The Breakfast Pops with Extra Pop!*

Letts Educational Ltd
The Chiswick Centre
414 Chiswick High Road
London W4 5TF
Telephone: 020 8996 3333
Fax: 020 8742 8390
e-mail: mail@lettsed.co.uk
website: www.letts-education.com

Letts Educational Limited is a division of Granada Learning Limited, part of Granada plc.

Also available from Letts

More essential reading from the brand leaders in home study

Achieve SATs success with our Key Stage 1 Success Guides available in Maths, English and Science.

Brightly coloured and easy to use revision guides

RRP: £3.50

Available at all good bookshops, or visit www.letts-education.com

To register and receive your free book simply log on to:

🖱 www.letts-education.com†

✉ or send your details‡ (Name, Age, School year, Address, Postcode, Email) to:
Free Book Offer, Letts Educational,
414 Chiswick High Road, London W4 5TF

† For e-mail registration: postage and packing payable as detailed on the website.
‡ For postal registrations: in order to receive your free book, please send a self addressed envelope with stamps to the value of £1.

Letts Educational reserve the right to close this promotion without prior notification. No purchase necessary.

FREE BOOK worth £3.50 or more when you register on our website today